PEARSON

Future Island

ACTIVITY BOOK

Contents

5

T0346224

WELCOME

1 (1:03) **Listen, say and match.**

advert *b* chimpanzee ___ nature reserve ___ guard ___ money ___ visitors ___

2 (1:04) **Listen and read. Then match.**

1 How much is that?
2 Can we take photographs of the animals?
3 He's cute! What's his name?
4 A family ticket is eight pounds, please.
5 His name is Champ.

3 **Look at the picture in Activity 1 and complete.**

1 Marta's dad has got a *nature reserve.*
2 Marta is carrying a _____.
3 The _____ is talking to two boys.
4 The _____ is for a funfair.
5 The _____ want to see the animals.

4 Look, read and complete.

> red   blue   moustache   money   trainers
> brown   nature reserve   friend   animals

1

2

3

Marta's got ___red___ hair. She loves _____. She helps her dad at the _____.

Chris is Marta's _____. He's got _____ hair. He's wearing _____.

Zero Zendell has got _____ hair and a _____. He's got a zoo. He loves _____.

5 (1:05) **Listen and say the years. Then work in pairs.**

A: 1
B: sixteen forty-two

1 1642   **2** 1462   **3** 1880

4 1980   **5** 1999   **6** 2001   **7** 2010   **8** 2210

6 (1:06) **Listen and match. Then say the years.**

1 20   **a** 10
2 19   **b** 05
3 20   **c** 75
4 20   **d** 65
5 19   **e** 50

1 Adventure camp

1 Look and match the names with the people.

| Hannah | ~~Tom~~ | Felipe | Flo | Maria |

a ___Tom___   b _____   c _____   d _____   e _____

2 Order the letters. Then match with the pictures.

1 **ttne**   ___tent___ c

2 **kkracsuc**   _____

3 **geps**   _____

4 **ctorh**   _____

5 **pomcssa**   _____

6 **isleengp gba** _____

3 (1:09) Look at Flo's list. Listen and tick (✓) or cross (✗).

List for Adventure Camp

rucksack	✓
torch	☐
pegs	☐
compass	☐
books	☐
mp3 player	☐
sleeping bag	☐

4 🔊 **1:10** **Read and choose. Then listen and check.**

1 I can *play* / *playing* football.
2 He likes *playing* / *play* computer games.
3 They are *Britain* / *British*.
4 We are good at *dancing* / *dance*.
5 She loves *trampoline* / *trampolining*.
6 He's good at *sing* / *singing*.

5 🔊 **1:11** **Look and match. Then listen and check.**

c — Lewis Hamilton
a — David Beckham
b — Taylor Swift
d — Penelope Cruz

1 🔑 is good at playing football. _____*a*_____
2 🔑 is good at acting and singing. _____
3 🔑 is from the USA and can play the guitar. _____
4 🔑 is British and loves fast cars. _____

6 **Choose a person from Activity 5 and write questions for them. Find out and write the answers.**

1 _____
2 _____
3 _____
4 _____

7 **Complete for you.**

My name's _____ I'm from _____
in _____
I love _____ and _____
but I don't like _____
I'm good at _____ and _____
but I'm not good at _____
I've got _____

8 Look and complete the sentences.

①  ②  ③

They're *pitching a tent.*   We're _____   He's _____

④  ⑤  ⑥

It's _____   I'm _____   He's _____

9 Look and write sentences.

1 The two boys ____*are pitching a tent.*____
2 The girl _____
3 The man _____
4 The two girls _____

10 (1:15) **Listen and answer.**

1 Who is the letter for?

_____

2 Is it Felipe's third day?

_____

3 What does Felipe want?

_____

11 (1:16) **Listen again and complete.**

Hello Grandad,   2nd July

How are you and ¹____Granny____? Adventure Camp is great. It's my fifth day here. I've got some new friends from ²_____ and Argentina. They're really nice. I'm teaching my new friend Flo, ³_____. She's funny and she's learning fast.

Our first day was good. There was a big dinner and then there were songs by the campfire. I don't like ⁴_____ but it was fun.

Yesterday, we ⁵_____ for a walk in the forest. It's very beautiful here but there ⁶_____ any computers and there isn't any internet! I want my computer games!
Love,
Felipe

12 **Imagine you're at Adventure Camp. Write a letter home.**

Dear _____,

How are you? Adventure Camp is _____
_____

Yesterday, _____
_____
_____

Love,

_____

13 Read and choose.

1 Marta and Chris are going:
a to the park.   b to the funfair.   c to school.

2 To go into the time machine costs:
a three dollars.   b ten dollars.   c a dollar.

3 Chris doesn't like:
a Zero Zendell.   b Marta.   c Champ.

4 Marta thinks the time machine is:
a scary.   b boring.   c cool.

5 At the end of the episode, Champ is:
a missing.   b in the time machine.   c in a tree.

14 Find and read Zero's code.

EHMYESGERCSSIT

TZIZ IZ MZ SZCZEZ MZSZAZE ZAZHZNZ.

This is my secret message machine.

15 Find and write. Then answer.

RAHCIP

WZEZE ZS ZHZMZ?

_____

_____

_____

_____

16 Look and write.

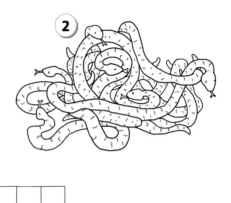
SOCIAL SCIENCE

1

①

②

Crossword:

```
            1                   2
            [ ]                 [ ]
              4
   3  [ ][ ][ ] n [ ][ ][ ][ ][ ]
            [ ]                 [ ]
   5  [ ][ ] i [ ][ ]  [ ]      k
            [ ]
                        6  i [ ][ ][ ][ ][ ]
```

③

④

⑤

⑥

17 Complete the sentences. Use words from Activity 16.

1 Bear likes playing the _____ *guitar.* _____
2 Bear sometimes lives in the _____.
3 There are often a lot of _____ in the jungle.
4 Bear sometimes sleeps up a _____ in the jungle.
5 His favourite place is an _____ in Indonesia.
6 Bear runs a lot and does _____.

18 **Look and write.**

Talking about loves

I **love**	
You **love**	play**ing** basketball.
He/She [1] *loves*	sing**ing**.
We **love**	talk**ing**.
They [2] _____	cook**ing**.

Talking about abilities

I'm/I'm **not**		swim**ming**.
You're/[3]_____		danc**ing**.
He's/He **isn't**	**good at**	surf**ing**.
She's/She **isn't**		sing**ing**.
We're/[4]_____		
They're/[5]_____		

Present continuous

I'm/[6]_____	
You're/You **aren't**	sit**ting**.
He's/He [7]_____	sleep**ing**.
She's/She **isn't**	cook**ing**.
We're/We **aren't**	pitch**ing** a tent.
They're/They [8]_____	

Do you like camping?

19 (1:19) **Read and complete the sentences. Then listen and check.**

play   loves   running   sometimes   doesn't   ~~good at~~

I've got two brothers, Peter and Patrick. They're very
different. Peter is [1] *good at* swimming and he
[2]_____ surfing. Patrick [3]_____ like water
but he loves camping and [4]_____. He's good at
skateboarding, too.
We often [5]_____ computer games at the weekend.
It's the one thing we all love and [6]_____ I win!

20 Complete the Unit Quiz.

Unit Quiz ? ? ? ? ?

1 Write six things to take camping.

_____

2 Order this sentence. (isn't) (Maria) (singing) (good) (at)

_____

3 Complete the sentences. Tick if they're true.
  a I _____ to the cinema yesterday. ☐
  b I like _____ football. ☐

4 Say this sentence fast.

The thirteen teachers think the time is two o'clock!

21 Write for you.

1 I love _____ and _____

2 I'm good at _____ but I'm not _____

3 Yesterday, I went _____
There were _____
_____
_____
_____

I CAN

☺ ☺ ☹

★ talk about camping.   ☐ ☐ ☐
★ talk about loves and abilities.   ☐ ☐ ☐
★ read, understand and write a letter.   ☐ ☐ ☐
★ spell and say the /θ/, /t/ and /ð/ sounds.   ☐ ☐ ☐
★ read about the adventurer Bear Grylls.   ☐ ☐ ☐

2 Wild animals

1 Look and write.

1
petelhna
elephant

2
hcthaee
_____

3
alkoa
_____

4
ksaen
_____

5
gefrifa
_____

6
poihp
_____

7
orinh
_____

8
ttoieros
_____

2 Write about the animals in Activity 1. Use these words.

~~heavy~~   long   tall   fast   slow

1 _____ _Elephants and rhinos are heavy._
2 _____
3 _____
4 _____
5 _____

3 🔊 1:23 Listen and say. Then match.

two thousand and ten   a   210
a hundred and eighty   b   1,018
two hundred and eighteen   c   218
two hundred and ten   d   2,010
a thousand and eighteen   e   180

4 (1:25) **Listen and complete the chart.**

| ~~1~~ 250 2.5 9 90 1.5 7 4 3,000 4,000 1 1.5 |

	How tall?	How heavy?	How long?
	_____ *1* _____ metre	_____ kilograms	3 metres
	_____ metre	60 kilograms	_____ metres
		_____ kilograms	_____ metres
	_____ metres	_____ kilograms	_____ metres
	_____ metres	_____ kilograms	_____ metres

5 **Find and write the questions.**

1 (is) (long) (how) (the) (hippo)

   How long is the hippo?

2 (tall) (how) (lion) (is) (the)

   _____

3 (the) (heavy) (how) (is) (snake)

   _____

4 (how) (elephant) (the) (is) (long)

   _____

6 **Write answers to the questions in Activity 5. Ask and answer.**

1 _____ _The hippo is 4 metres long._ _____

2 _____

3 _____

4 _____

7 Complete the table. Use these words.

~~fast~~   heavy   small   long   short   slow   hot   tall   wet

big → big**ger** than
_____
_____

happy → happ**ier** than
_____

cold → cold**er** than
faster than
_____
_____
_____
_____
_____
_____

8 Look and make sentences.

long   big   heavy   ~~fast~~   slow

1 The lemur *is faster than the tiger.*
2 The panther _____
3 The whale _____
4 The whale _____
5 The tortoise _____

9 Write the questions. Then write the answers.

1 panther/fast/lemur   *Is the panther faster than the lemur?*
_____*No, it isn't.*_____

2 seal/long/whale   _____
_____

3 tortoise/fast/otter   _____
_____

4 whale/heavy/turtle   _____
_____

5 lemur/fast/tiger   _____
_____

10 (1:29) **Listen to the interview with Jen from the Koala Reserve and choose.**

1 Mike *likes* / *doesn't like* the Koala Reserve.
2 Vernie is *7 metres* / *70 centimetres* tall.
3 Vernie likes *running* / *sleeping*.
4 Mike wants to sponsor *Jen* / *Vernie*.

11 (1:30) **Listen again and order Mike's questions. Then write the answers.**

a How tall is Vernie? ☐ _____

b Can I ask you some questions? 1 _____ *Of course!* _____

c How heavy is she? ☐ _____

d How fast is she? ☐ _____

12 **Complete. Then circle.**

1 Giraffes are __taller__ (tall) than lions.　(True) False Sometimes true
2 Rhinos are _____ (heavy) than otters.　True False Sometimes true
3 Cheetahs are _____ (short) than elephants.　True False Sometimes true
4 Turtles are _____ (big) than whales.　True False Sometimes true
5 Tortoises are _____ (fast) than tigers.　True False Sometimes true
6 Crocodiles are _____ (long) than snakes.　True False Sometimes true
7 Elephants are _____ (slow) than cheetahs.　True False Sometimes true
8 Seals are _____ (small) than rabbits.　True False Sometimes true

13 (1:31) **Listen and circle the correct sound. Then complete the sentence with the circled letters.**

1 (v) w
2 v w
3 v w
4 v w
5 v w
6 v w

I lo*v*e _et _eather in the _inter but _ernie _ants an umbrella!

14 Read and complete.

This is ^{1}_____. She's got ^{2}_____
hair and she's ^{3}_____ funny clothes.
She is Chris and Marta's new ^{4}_____.

15 (1:33) Find and correct seven errors. Then listen and check.

Marta and Chris meet (Sarah). She thinks they are poor because they have got a cat.
Zero Zendell wants animals at any time. The children are in a nature park. The guards
look after them. Sarah wants to help Marta and Chris.

16 (1:34) Listen and complete the rules at the nature museum.

NATURE MUSEUM

1 Don't sit *on the grass.*
2 Don't _____ in the museum.
3 Don't _____ the _____.
4 Don't give food or _____ to the animals.
5 Don't take _____ of the animals.

RULES

17 Look at page 8. Find and write. Then do.

CTRERUFRORROLTE

WZIZE ZHZEZ RZLZS ZOZ YZUZ
SZHZOZ.

I _____

2 _____

3 _____

18 Read. When do Arctic foxes have white/brown coats?

SEARCH

Cool camouflage in the cold!

Size They're not very heavy and they're not very big. Their tails are usually about 30 centimetres long.

Body Arctic foxes have got short legs and short ears. Their coats and tails are very thick and warm – good for living in the snow!

Colour Arctic foxes' coats are very good camouflage. Their coats are white when it is snowy in the winter. In the summer, their coats are darker and change to brown or grey. It's difficult to see the foxes next to the brown rocks.

Places Arctic foxes live only in the Arctic, for example in Canada and Greenland. It is very cold there. They can live in temperatures of -50 degrees Celsius.

Food Arctic foxes eat birds, fish and sometimes vegetables. They're good at catching birds – they're very fast! They often put food in the snow and then eat it later in the year.

19 Read the sentences and write *C* (chameleon) or *F* (fox).

1 This animal changes colour when it's nervous. _C_

2 This animal lives in very cold places. ___

3 This animal sometimes eats fish. ___

4 This animal has got a very long tongue. ___

20 Think about a wild animal. Draw and complete the profile.

Animal	
Size	
Body	
Colour	
Places	
Food	

21 Look and write.

Asking for measurements

| How [1] _tall_ is the giraffe? | It's 5 metres tall. |
| How [2] _____ is the hippo? | It's 3,000 kilograms. |

How long is it? How tall is it? How heavy is it? And how clever is it?!

Comparing two things

The cat is	tall	→	**tall**er **than**	the tortoise.
	long	→	3 _____	
	heavy	→	4 _____	
	fast	→	5 _____	

22 (1:36) Read and write. Then listen and check.

> bigger   longer   ~~was~~   bigger   were   was

20th July

We went to the wildlife park yesterday. There
[1] ___was___ a hippo and its name was Henry. It
[2] _____ very old but its mouth was [3] _____
than an elephant's mouth and its body was [4] _____ than
a giraffe's body.

Henry's teeth [5] _____ very big! They were [6] _____ than my teeth!

Flo

23 Complete the Unit Quiz.

Unit Quiz

1 Name five wild animals.

2 Write the correct questions.

a _____ A giraffe is 5 metres tall.

b _____ An elephant is 7 metres long.

c _____ A koala is 8 kilograms.

3 What does 'camouflage' mean?

a a type of animal   **b** using pattern and colour to hide   **c** a type of tree

4 Say 'w' and 'v' fast, then faster, then faster!

24 Write about your favourite animal.

My favourite animal is _____

_____

_____

_____

_____

_____

I CAN

★ say the names of a lot of animals in English.

★ say and ask how tall/heavy/long/fast animals are.

★ compare two different things.

★ talk about animal life and the natural world.

★ spell and say the /v/ and /w/ sounds.

★ talk about animals and camouflage.

3 Where I live

1 Find and write.

shopping centre

s	h	o	p	p	i	n	g	c	e	n	t	r	e	c
a	z	e	g	j	l	j	u	o	h	y	w	r	k	a
f	c	l	i	b	r	a	r	y	y	r	k	h	k	s
z	i	d	h	y	k	r	d	f	q	z	o	t	p	t
x	n	s	u	p	e	r	m	a	r	k	e	t	a	l
y	e	g	h	j	y	g	c	c	x	z	a	t	r	e
p	m	v	b	b	n	m	p	o	u	y	r	e	k	q
g	a	h	g	g	h	j	k	l	o	i	y	w	b	u
s	w	i	m	m	i	n	g	p	o	o	l	d	c	p

2 Complete with the places in Activity 1.

1 I can buy some clothes in a _____ _shopping centre._ _____
2 I can find interesting books in a _____.
3 I can see the town from a _____.
4 I can play football in a _____.
5 I can dive in a _____.
6 I can watch a film in a _____.
7 I can buy juice in a _____.

3 Read and answer about you.

1 Where do you like going? _____
2 What can you do there? _____
3 What do you like doing there? _____

4 Look and write. Where is the ice cream van?

in front of   next to   ~~between~~   opposite   behind   near

between

_____

_____

_____

_____

_____

5 1:41 Listen and complete the map.

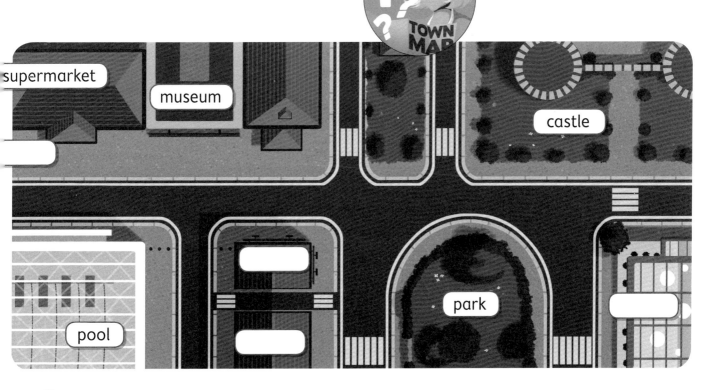

6 Look at the map in Activity 5 and write sentences in your notebook.

The supermarket is near the cinema.

7 Look and write. Then match.

a s u n s e t

b __ a __ __ __

c s __ __ __

d __ i __ __ __

e t __ __ __ __ __

f __ __ o __ __ __ __

1 Have you got an umbrella?

2 It's quiet here – I like it!

3 Look at the bird!

4 It's beautiful. Look at the red and yellow colours.

5 It's too noisy for me!

6 Oh, no! Where's the sun?

8 Look and write.

1 Tom/go/the park ✗
  Tom doesn't want to go to the park.

2 Flo/be/a film star ✓
  _____

3 Felipe/buy/a computer game ✓
  _____

4 Maria/play/basketball ✗
  _____

9 1:44 Look at Activity 8 and write dialogues. Then listen and check.

1 Hi, Tom. Do you want to go to the park?   No, I don't! I want to go to the beach.

2 _____   _____

3 _____   _____

4 _____   _____

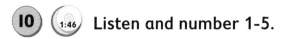
10 (1:46) **Listen and number 1-5.**

a   Do you want to come to Liverpool in the summer? ☐

b   I don't like quiet places! ☐

c   I live near a big park with a lot of trees and flowers. ☐

d   My school's nice and I'm very happy there. ☐

e   Thanks for your email. It was really interesting! 1

Alex

Jack

11 (1:47) **Choose the correct answer. Listen again and check.**

1   Alex **wants** / **doesn't want** to know more about Liverpool.

2   Jack **likes** / **doesn't like** quiet places.

3   There's a river **near** / **behind** Jack's house.

4   Jack **wants** / **doesn't want** to go to Sark one day.

12 **Read and write and, but or because.**

1   I don't like the city __because__ it's too noisy.

2   I like surfing _____ snorkelling.

3   He likes going to the library _____ he doesn't like going to the castle.

4   My village is clean _____ it isn't beautiful.

5   She wants to go to bed _____ she's tired.

13 **Write three sentences about where you live.**

I like my city because _____

In _____ there are _____ and _____

There are _____ but there aren't any _____

14 **Read and answer.** *True* **or** *false*?

    1 Serena opens the door with a key. _____*False*_____

    2 Serena has got a pet cat. _____

    3 There aren't any real pets in the future. _____

    4 Zero Zendell has got a zoo. _____

    5 Chris and Marta don't want to rescue Champ. _____

15 **Look at the picture of Serena's house. Read and draw.**

Hi! This is where I live. It's in a noisy, busy city but I like it. My favourite thing in the house is the sofa. There's a TV opposite the sofa. I love sitting on the sofa and watching TV in the evening. There's a small table between the sofa and the TV. My dinner is on the table – it's fish and chips. I've got cupboards and a tall lamp in my room, too. The lamp is between the cupboards and the sofa. There's a picture behind the lamp, on the wall. It's a picture of some beautiful flowers. My bed is near the table and the sofa but it's not near the cupboards. But where's my robot dog? Oh, there he is! He's in front of my bed. He's hiding!

16 **Look at page 8. Find and write. Then do.**

T R O R E O D R W T A O T A R

D■A■ Y■U■ B■D■O■M ■N■ W■I■E ■B■U■ I■.

17 Look and write. Then guess the countries.

chimney bridge hill river roof

1 *chimney*

2

3

18 (1:50) **Match the paragraphs with the pictures and write the words. Then listen and check.**

Australia because bridge houses near next park village want

☐ Upper Swell is a pretty ¹____*village*____ in Britain. It's got a lot of old
²_____. There is also a river in the village with a
³_____. It's very quiet but a lot of people visit it in the summer.

☐ The Adelaide Hills are in ⁴_____. It's very lovely there. You can
see a lot of animals and birds in the wildlife ⁵_____. The hills are
⁶_____ the city of Adelaide.

☐ Barcelona is a big city in Spain, ⁷_____ to the sea. Tourists
⁸_____ to go there ⁹_____ there is always a lot to do
and see. This interesting building is by Gaudi.

19 Think about a place you know in your country. Write in your notebook.

20 Look and write.

Talking about what I want to do

I/You **want to/don't want to** He/She [1] _____wants_____ **to/doesn't want to** We/They [2] _____ /[3] _____	live in a city. watch the sunset. go to the park.
Do you **want to** go to the pool? Yes, I **do**./No, I [4] _____ .	

Talking about position

5 _opposite_

7 _____

6 _____

8 _____

Do you want to go to the pool?

21 Read the email and write.

~~near~~ park quiet noisy want shopping centre between

Hi!

I'm Flo! I'm looking for an e-pal in a big city.

I live in a small town in England. My friends live [1] _____near_____ my house and there's a park [2] _____ my house and the school. In summer, we eat a lot of ice cream and play football in the [3] _____ . In winter, we can go to the [4] _____ or the cinema.

There aren't a lot of cars and buses on the streets in my town and there aren't a lot of people. My town's quite boring – it's too small and [5] _____ .
I [6] _____ to live in a big, [7] _____ city!

Please write and tell me about big city life soon.

Flo

22 Complete the Unit Quiz.

Unit Quiz

1 Say the names of six places in a town.

2 Complete these words. Then draw pictures in your notebook.

a b__t__een   **b** o__po__i__e   **c** n___ __r   **d** b__h__n__

3 Write three places you want to go to.

a _____   **c** _____

b _____

4 Write two sentences. Use *and*, *but* and *because*.

_____

_____

23 Write about your town/city.

_____

_____

_____

_____

_____

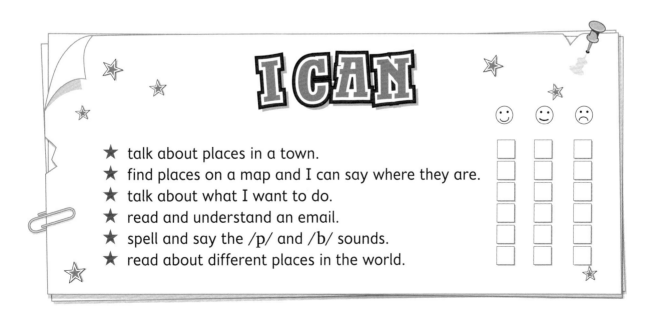

I CAN

☺ ☺ ☹

★ talk about places in a town.

★ find places on a map and I can say where they are.

★ talk about what I want to do.

★ read and understand an email.

★ spell and say the /p/ and /b/ sounds.

★ read about different places in the world.

1 Look and write. What is Flo's favourite food?

My favourite food is _____.

1 | s | | | g | | | | |

2 | | m | | | | | |

4   5   6

3 | | | | | | n | | | | |

                     r

2 Complete the quiz. Use the food in Activity 1.

Quiz

1 ___Omelettes___ are French.
2 _____ is Spanish.
3 _____ is Italian.
4 _____ is Indian.
5 _____ is British.

3 Make a list of food you like and don't like. Tell a friend.

I like _____

_____

I don't like _____

_____

4 Find five words.

missedrpeclimbedibwantedruycookedtqadropped

5 Complete. Use the words in Activity 4.

1 Last year I _____wanted_____ to be a doctor but now I'm not sure.

2 We _____ paella yesterday. It was difficult!

3 I _____ Mount Everest last year.

4 He _____ the plate on his foot. Ouch!

6 Read and write. Who is the writer? Tom, Flo or Felipe?

loved   enjoy   was   ~~went~~   paddled   wanted   were

Yesterday was a good day. A lot of people ¹___went___ to the lake to do sports and I went with them. There was swimming, snorkelling and kayaking. I ²_____ scared at first but I ³_____ kayaking. It was amazing! I ⁴_____ to do it all day. I was with Tom and we ⁵_____ very fast around the lake. There was a race with Flo and Maria and we were the winners.

After our day at the lake, there ⁶_____ omelettes and salad for dinner. I didn't ⁷_____ the omelette. I prefer paella!

7 Look and match.

miss   pack   open

pass   drop

a the ball
b my bag
c the bus
d a lunchbox
e a test

8 (2:06) Read and choose. Then listen and check.

1   I **wanted** / **didn't want** a salad but there weren't any tomatoes.
2   They **remembered** / **didn't remember** their sandwiches but they remembered the apples.
3   Flo **missed** / **didn't miss** the bus yesterday. She was early.
4   Tom **dropped** / **didn't drop** the ball. He was the winner.
5   I **opened** / **didn't open** the window because it was hot.

9 Look and complete the sentences.

~~drop~~   love   play   like   want

1 There was a lot of food on her tray but she _didn't drop_ her lunch.

2 The woman _____ the film but the boys _____ it.

3 He _____ football last week. He was sad because he really _____ to play.

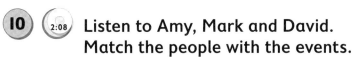

10 (2:08) **Listen to Amy, Mark and David. Match the people with the events.**

 Amy

 Mark

 David

1 a holiday _____

2 a party _____

3 a test _____

11 (2:09) **Listen again and choose.**

1 Amy didn't want:
  a a big cake.   **b** a big party.   **c** a surprise party.

2 Amy's mum cooked:
  a omelettes.   **b** a curry.   **c** spaghetti.

3 Mark did a _____ test.
  a Geography   **b** Spanish   **c** Maths

4 Mark's friends:
  a passed the test, too.   **b** didn't pass the test.   **c** missed the test.

5 David went:
  a swimming and sailing.   **b** swimming and surfing.   **c** swimming and kayaking.

12 **Write about a good day last year.**

A good day last year was _____
_____
_____
_____

It was great because _____
_____
_____
_____

13 (2:10) **Listen and write.**

1 He _____*wanted*_____ to go to the park.

2 They always _____ dinner at six o'clock.

3 I _____ the film but it was too long.

4 We always _____ our tests because we always do our homework.

5 She _____ the bus because she was late.

14 Correct the sentences.

1 Serena didn't visit the zoo last year.   _Serena visited the zoo last year._
2 She liked the zoo.   _____
3 Serena didn't climb onto the roof.   _____
4 The assistant didn't lock Champ's cage.   _____
5 Champ didn't open the cage.   _____
6 Serena wasn't in danger.   _____

15 Look and complete. Use these words.

open lock drop laugh climb

He _opened_ his cage.

He _____ onto the table.

He _____ a chair on my head.

He _____ me in the cage.

He _____ at me.

16 Look at page 8. Find and write. Then do.

R O I E O A I E A E E A R T T T A E A

Z M Z G Z N Z Y Z U Z R Z S Z R Z N Z.
W Z I Z E Z B Z U Z Y Z S Z E Z D Z Y.

_____
_____
_____
_____

17 Look and complete the lists. Then write one more.

> dangerous   filmed   sixth

1 sailed, started, finished, phoned, enjoyed, _____ _____
2 first, second, third, fourth, fifth, _____ _____
3 scary, brave, boring, tired, sad, _____ _____

18 (2:13) Look and complete Ellen's diary. Then listen and check.

1st January

Yesterday was a really good day. There were no ¹ _____*storms*_____

and the weather was good. I was ² ☺ _____ because I

³ _____ my family and friends. I ⁴ _____

my Christmas presents, too. I ⁵ ♥ _____ the funny presents and

the ⁶ _____.

19 Imagine you're a sailor or adventurer. Write a diary. Use these words.

> sea   storm   happy   sad   scary   exciting   animals   jungle   mountains

Yesterday was a good day _____
_____
_____
_____

20 Look and write.

Talking about the past

| I/You
He/She
We/They | dance**d**/**didn't dance** at the party.
like**d**/¹ _____*didn't like*_____ the ice cream.
drop**ped**/**didn't drop** the plate.
play**ed**/² _____ football.
walk**ed**/³ _____ to the park. |

Builder Bill danced all night at the party!

21 Write the verbs in the correct column.

~~dance~~   laugh   remember   love   stop   talk   pack   smile   climb   phone

look – look**ed**	like – like**d**	drop – drop**ped**
_____	*danced*	_____
_____	_____	_____
_____	_____	_____
_____	_____	_____

22 Write these sentences in a different way.

1 ✓ I liked the film last night. ✗ _____*I didn't like the film last night.*_____

2 ✗ He didn't climb a mountain last year. ✓ _____*He climbed a mountain last year.*_____

3 ✗ Yesterday, we didn't stay at the library all afternoon. ✓ _____
_____

4 ✓ James visited his grandparents last Saturday. ✗ _____
_____

5 ✗ Sally didn't walk to school yesterday. ✓ _____

23 **Complete the Unit Quiz.**

Unit Quiz ? ? ? ? ? ?

1 Where are these international foods from?
  a paella _____   **b** fish and chips _____   **c** curry _____

2 Write this sentence in a different way.
  ✗ He didn't want to go to the party. ✓ _____

3 Read and choose for you.
  I *played / didn't play* football yesterday.

4 Say this sentence, then faster, then faster!

> Donny wanted the ball but he passed it on to Ted, Ted played fast but it bounced off the teacher's head!

24 **Write five sentences about last weekend or last night.**

Last _____

_____

_____

_____

_____

I CAN

☺ ☺ ☹

★ name some international food.
★ talk about things in the past.
★ read, understand and write about a good day.
★ spell and say verbs in the past.
★ read about the sailor Ellen MacArthur.

5 Trips

1 Look and write.

1 ___aquarium___

2 _____

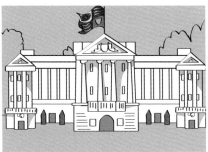

3 _____

4 _____

5 _____

6 _____

2 (2:16) Read and complete with words from Activity 1. Then listen and check.

1 We went to the ___aquarium___. There were a lot of fish there.
2 We loved the _____ because we love swimming.
3 I liked the _____. The actors were very good.
4 The _____ was fun but the Queen wasn't there.
5 The _____ was good fun. I was sometimes scared but it was exciting!
6 The _____ was OK but I don't really like old pictures.

3 Complete for you. Use words from Activity 1.

I love going to _____ and _____
I like _____
but I don't _____

4 (2:18) **Look and complete. Then listen and check.**

> ~~went~~ Did didn't go didn't

1 I ___*went*___ to the cinema last week.
2 They _____ go to the theme park on Saturday.
3 _____ she go to the swimming pool? No, she _____.
4 He didn't _____ to the park yesterday.

5 **Find and write.**

1 (the) (yesterday) (did) (go) (you) (to) (supermarket)

   Did you go to the supermarket yesterday?

2 (on) (the) (didn't) (park) (I) (go) (to) (Saturday)

   _____.

3 (went) (ago) (she) (swimming) (pool) (the) (to) (days) (two)

   _____.

4 (they) (library) (the) (week) (last) (did) (go) (to)

   _____?

5 (we) (a) (in) (park) (to) (2009) (went) (theme)

   _____.

6 (2:19) **Listen and tick (✓) or cross (✗). Then write questions and answers.**

① ② ③ ④ ⑤ ⑥

✓ ☐ ☐ ☐ ☐ ☐

1 ___*Did Maria go to the palace?*___   *Yes, she did.*
2 _____   _____
3 _____   _____
4 _____   _____
5 _____   _____
6 _____   _____

7 Look and find these five words.

①

big wheel

b	o	a	t	i	n	g	l	a	k	e	b	k
m	q	e	r	y	u	i	k	o	b	f	o	a
i	g	k	t	s	f	i	q	d	i	v	a	n
n	z	f	r	b	m	u	k	r	g	m	c	i
i	d	o	d	g	e	m	s	i	w	x	a	m
g	z	x	w	g	r	d	a	z	h	t	r	g
o	s	h	u	w	t	x	i	w	e	q	o	d
l	c	a	r	o	u	s	e	l	e	z	o	o
f	x	j	t	g	z	r	w	d	l	n	a	d
r	o	l	l	e	r	c	o	a	s	t	e	r

⑤

_____

②

_____

③

_____

④

_____

8 Find the sixth word. Then complete Felipe's sentence.

My favourite ride in a theme park is the _____.

9 Look and match.

1 play — a TV/a comedy/a thriller
2 like b to pop music/at a disco
3 watch c trampolining/chocolate cake/diving
4 dance d basketball/computer games/chess

10 Complete the questions. Then match with the answers.

1 Did you __*like*__ the chocolate cake?
2 Did we _____ football last week?
3 Did she _____ the aquarium?
4 Did he _____ a funny film?
5 Did you _____ at the school disco?

a Yes, I did. I'm tired now!
b No, he didn't. He watched a scary film.
c Yes, she did. She loved the fish.
d No, we didn't. It was too rainy.
e Yes, I did. I love chocolate!

11 (2:23) Listen and complete the brochure.

Come to Blackpool!

We've got ¹ _long_ , sandy beaches!
Visit the famous ² _____!
Go snorkelling and ³ _____!
In the evening, go ⁴ _____
or ⁵ _____!
You're never bored in Blackpool!

13 Imagine you went to the beach last summer. Write an email.

From: _____
To: _____
Subject: _____

Hi _____

I'm in _____
_____
_____
_____
_____
_____

Love,
_____

12 (2:24) Listen and choose.

Oliver

1 Oliver went to the
  water park / *theme park*.
2 The rides were *boring* / *exciting*.
3 The weather was *rainy* / *sunny*.
4 Oliver went *trampolining* / *ice-skating*.
5 He *loved* / *didn't like* Blackpool.

14 (2:25) Listen and mark the stress.

1 water park
2 swimming pool
3 shopping centre
4 theme park
5 big wheel

15 **Read and complete.**

> ~~closed~~   zoo   river   started   easy

1 The nature reserve _____closed_____ 100 years ago.
2 Marta's parents _____ the nature reserve.
3 There was an underground _____.
4 It was _____ to bring food for the animals.
5 The river went past the _____ and into the nature reserve.

16 (2:27) **Listen and match.**

1 water park _____   3 aquarium _____
2 palace _____   4 theme park _____

17 **Look at page 8. Find and write. Then do.**

T R H S E T O A A O R O S D D

WℤAT'ℤ NℤXℤ Tℤ YℤUℤ
HℤUℤE? ℤRℤW ℤNℤ WℤIℤE.

18 Read and do the quiz. What's your score?

How beach-safe are you?

1 You are swimming. You swim between the:
  a black and white flags.
  b black and blue flags.
  c red and yellow flags.

2 You are on the beach and it's very sunny. You:
  a wear sun cream.
  b wear ice cream.
  c wear your favourite jeans.

3 You are swimming in the sea. You:
  a always swim far from the beach.
  b always swim near the beach.
  c never swim near the beach.

4 You are surfing. You surf between the:
  a black and white flags.
  b red and yellow flags.
  c black and blue flags.

5 You are surfing in the sea. Your surfboard is always:
  a on the beach.
  b next to you.
  c far from you.

0-5 points – Oh no! Don't go to the beach!
10-15 points – You are quite safe but read the rules again!
20-25 points – You are very safe on the beach!
5 a 0 points b 5 points c 0 points
4 a 5 points b 0 points c 0 points
3 a 0 points b 5 points c 0 points
2 a 5 points b 0 points c 0 points
1 a 0 points b 0 points c 5 points

19 Look and write in the correct column(s).

| snorkelling | rollerblading | surfing | horse-riding |
| walking | diving | skateboarding | climbing |

snorkelling		

20 **Look and write.**

Asking about the past

1 _____	I you he/she/we/they	**go** to the palace? **like** the museum? **dance** in the rain?
Yes, I **did**./No, I 2 _____ .		

I/You He/She We/They	**didn't go** to the palace. 3 _____ **like** the weather. 4 _____ **watch** the film.

I didn't dance in the rain!

21 (2:29) **Number. Then listen and check.**

a   No, I didn't. The water was cold. ☐
b   Yes, we did but the ball went into the water! ☐
c   Did you go to the beach on Saturday? ☐1
d   Yes, I did. We went swimming in the sea. ☐
e   Did you like it? ☐
f   Did you play football on the beach? ☐

I CAN DO IT!

22 **Complete the Unit Quiz.**

Unit Quiz ? ? ? ? ? ?

1 Complete these places.
a __ a l a __ __ __   **b** __ q __ __ __ r i __ m   **c** t __ e __ t __ e
d w __ t __ __ __ __ __ r k

2 Write three things in a theme park. **a** _____ **b** _____ **c** _____

3 Order the question.

(you) (did) (go) (park) (to) (the) (yesterday)

_____

4 Write your answer to Question 3.

_____

23 **Write six sentences about last year and last week.**

Last year, I _____
_____
_____

Last week, _____
_____
_____

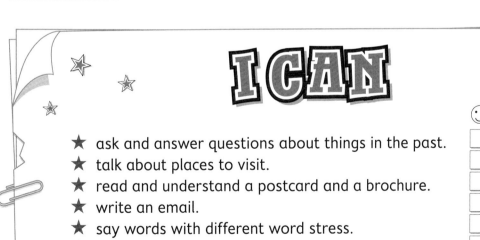

I CAN

☺ ☺ ☹

★ ask and answer questions about things in the past.
★ talk about places to visit.
★ read and understand a postcard and a brochure.
★ write an email.
★ say words with different word stress.
★ read about beach safety.

1 Look and write.

sci-fi ~~musical~~ cartoon romance thriller comedy

1

musical

2

_____

3

_____

4

_____

5

_____

6

_____

2 2:33 Listen to Maria and Felipe and choose.

1 Maria likes **romances / thrillers** because they are exciting.
2 She thinks she's too old for **cartoons / musicals** now.
3 Felipe loves **comedies / cartoons**.
4 He doesn't like **musicals / comedies**.

3 Complete the sentences for you.

I like _____ _cartoons_ _____ and _____ but I don't like

_____

I love _____ because _____

4 **Look and write. What did/didn't they do last week?**

1 Tom ✗ make   *Tom didn't make a cake last week.*

2 Maria ✓ see   SHADOW IN THE KITCHEN   _____

3 Felipe ✓ have   _____

4 Flo ✗ write in   Flo's diary   _____

5 Maria and Flo ✗ go   _____

5 (2:35) **Complete Flo's diary. Then listen and check.**

~~was~~   didn't see   made   saw   had   said   went   said

17th July

Yesterday ¹__was__ fun. I ²_____ to the cinema.
Maria went too but she saw a thriller. I ³_____
a comedy. It was about a funny man, George. He
⁴_____ a lot of funny noises and I ⁵_____ a good
time. After the film, I saw Maria but she ⁶_____ me. I
⁷_____, 'Boo!' She was scared! It was funny but I
⁸_____,'Sorry' and we laughed.

6 **Write about last weekend. Write three sentences.**

Last Saturday, _____

_____

_____

7 Find ten music words. Complete the table.

s	p	i	a	n	o	z	r	t	p
a	z	x	g	u	i	t	a	r	o
x	d	v	i	o	l	i	n	o	p
o	h	a	r	m	o	n	i	c	a
p	x	v	b	r	o	c	k	z	o
h	v	w	l	x	d	z	v	j	t
o	m	q	u	z	r	w	q	a	z
n	z	v	e	x	u	w	k	z	v
e	w	x	s	q	m	z	j	z	m

SONG

Instruments	Music styles
piano	_____
_____	_____
_____	_____
_____	_____
_____	

8 (2:40) Read and write. Then listen and check.

> did   violins   ~~Did~~   rock   was   hear   didn't

Jon: Hi, Sally. ¹_____*Did*_____ you go to a concert on Saturday?

Sally: Yes, I ²_____. It ³_____ amazing!

Jon: Really? Did you ⁴_____ any pianos?

Sally: Pianos? No, I didn't.

Jon: Oh … did you see any ⁵_____?

Sally: No, I ⁶_____. But I saw guitars.
It was a ⁷_____ concert!

9 Write four questions for a friend. Write the answers.

1 _____ _____
2 _____ _____
3 _____ _____
4 _____ _____

10 (2:42) **Listen and choose.**

1 Alicia is talking about:
a a song.   **b** a book.

2 Its name is:
a *Inkheart.*   **b** *Inkeyes.*

Alicia

11 (2:43) **Listen again and tick (✓).**

		True	False	Don't know
1	It's about a girl, Meggie.	✓		
2	Meggie and her dad love books.			
3	The monsters are scary.			
4	Meggie and Alicia are twelve.			
5	Alicia didn't like the film.			

12 **Write a review of your favourite book. Think about the characters, story and why you like it.**

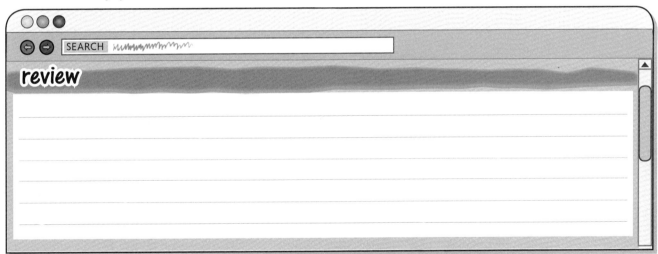

SEARCH

review

13 (2:44) **Complete. Use these words. Then listen and repeat.**

drawing   ~~saw~~   wrote   go   small   boat

1 Yesterday, I _____*saw*_____ a comedy in the cinema.
2 This T-shirt is too _____!
3 He's _____ a _____ on the sea.
4 She _____ a letter to her granny last night.
5 I usually _____ to the shopping centre on Saturdays.

14 (2:46) **Listen and complete Zero's advert.**

1

Last year, I _crossed_ the sea to South America.

2

I _____ a mountain.

3

I _____ into the rainforest.

4

I _____ a very tall tree.

5

I _____ a special cage.

6

And I _____ the last dodo in the world!

15 **Zero Zendell's sentences are not true. He bought the dodo! Correct the sentences.**

1 _____ _He didn't cross the sea to South America._
2 _____
3 _____
4 _____
5 _____
6 _____

16 **Look at page 8. Find and write. Then answer.**

H H S E O O E L T U

D⚡E⚡ Z⚡R⚡ T⚡L⚡ T⚡E ⚡R⚡T⚡?

_____
_____
_____
_____

17 Find and circle ten words.

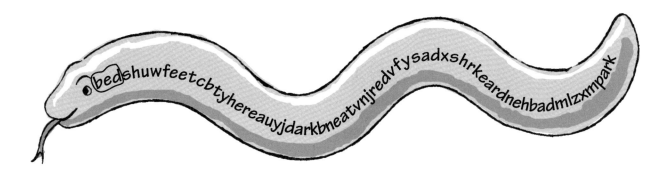

bed shuwfeetcbtyhereauyjdarkbneatvnjredvfysadxshrkeardnehbadmlzxmpark

18 (2:48) Put the words into rhyming pairs. Then listen and check.

1 _____bed_____ _____
2 _____ _____
3 _____ _____
4 _____ _____
5 _____ _____

19 Imagine you meet an animal or a monster. In pairs, write a poem. Use rhyming words.

20 **Look and write.**

Talking about the past

have	→	¹ _had_	→	didn't have
hear	→	**heard**	→	⁵ _____
make	→	² _____	→	didn't make
see	→	³ _____	→	didn't see
write	→	**wrote**	→	⁶ _____
say	→	⁴ _____	→	didn't say

Did you hear the cat?

No, I didn't.

Asking about the past

| Did | you **see** the concert? | Yes, I **did**.
No, I **didn't**. |
| | they **hear** the piano? | Yes, they ⁷ _____.
No, they ⁸ _____. |

21 (2:49) **Listen and tick (✓). Then complete Flo's diary.**

	make a cake	write a birthday card	say 'Happy Birthday'	have tickets for *Cats*	see the dancers
Flo					
Tom					
Mum	✓				

My birthday last year was great. My ¹ _mum_ made a cake for me.
Tom ² _____ a nice birthday card and everyone ³ _____ 'Happy Birthday!'
I was very happy. Mum ⁴ _____ tickets for *Cats* and Mum and I ⁵ _____ the
next day. We ⁶ _____ the dancers and ⁷ _____ some great music. I loved it!

50 **Round-up**

22 Complete the Unit Quiz.

I CAN DO IT!

Unit Quiz

1 What type of film is:
   a *Shadow in the House?*   **b** *Love in Paris?*   **c** *Monkeys in Space?*

   _____   _____   _____

2 Change the words.
   a made   →   _____   **c** had   →   _____
   b wrote   →   _____   **d** said   →   _____

3 Write three musical instruments.
   a _____   **b** _____   **c** _____

4 Order the words. Then answer the question.

   [you] [birthday] [did] [a] [party] [have] [month] [last]

   _____

5 Say this sentence fast!

   She saw a small yellow coat on a tall goat.

23 Complete these sentences for you.

1 My favourite music is _____ but I don't like _____
2 I can play the _____ but I can't play the _____
3 Last month, I _____
4 Last year, I _____

I CAN

⭐ talk about types of films.
⭐ talk about the past.
⭐ talk about music.
⭐ read, understand and write a book review.
⭐ spell and say the /ɔː/ and /əʊ/ sounds.
⭐ read a poem in English.

7 Space

1 **Match the word halves. Then write.**

① tele   ② astro   ③ space   ens   rs   on

④ Mo   ⑤ pla   ⑥ sta   ⑦ ali   naut   ship   net   scope

1 _____telescope_____   5 _____

2 _____   6 _____

3 _____   7 _____

4 _____

2 (3:03) **Look at the solar system and match. Then listen and check.**

Mercury   Jupiter   Uranus   Earth   SUN   Venus   Mars   Saturn   Neptune

1   Mars is the   **a**   third planet from the Sun.
2   Earth is the   **b**   second planet from the Sun.
3   Jupiter is the   **c**   eighth planet from the Sun.
4   Neptune is the   **d**   fifth planet from the Sun.
5   Venus is the   **e**   fourth planet from the Sun.

3 Look and complete the sentences.

1 The astronaut is in _____the spaceship._____
2 The astronaut is angry because there are _____ in the spaceship.
3 Alien a has got _____.
4 Alien b is _____ on the astronaut's spacesuit.

4 Find and write the questions. Match with the sentences in Activity 3.

1 (a) (telescope) (who) (got) (has)   _Who has got a telescope? 3_

2 (the) (is) (astronaut) (where)   _____

3 (why) (astronaut) (the) (is) (angry)   _____

4 (doing) (alien) (what's) (b)   _____

5 Write five questions for a friend. Ask the questions and write the answers.

1 What's _____your mum's name?_____   _____
2 Who _____   _____
3 Where _____   _____
4 When _____   _____
5 Why _____   _____

6 Complete the table. Use these words.

~~big~~ ~~amazing~~ exciting   difficult   scary   tall   clever   easy
frightening   complicated   small   intelligent

One or two syllables	Three syllables or more
big	*amazing*

7 Read and tick (✓) or cross (✗) for you. Then ask a friend.

	You	A friend
1 Thrillers are scarier than cartoons.	☐	☐
2 Football is more interesting than basketball.	☐	☐
3 Theme parks are more exciting than libraries.	☐	☐
4 Elephants are more frightening than tigers.	☐	☐
5 Art is more complicated than English.	☐	☐

8 Find and complete the sentences. Then write *Y* for *Yes* or *N* for *No*.

1 (more) (interesting) (than) (are) (films)

Books _____*are more interesting than films.*_____ ☐

2 (beautiful) (than) (more) (is) (planets) (other)

The Earth _____ ☐

3 (more) (has) (got) (an actor) (a) (dangerous) (job) (than)

A firefighter _____ ☐

4 (more) (are) (snakes) (than) (frightening)

Aliens _____ ☐

5 (than) (more) (English) (is) (difficult)

Science _____ ☐

9 (3:08) Connor is reading the second part of his story. Listen and tick (✓).

10 (3:09) Listen again and number the sentences.

a The aliens said, 'Thank you!' to Jake. ☐   **c** There were some small green aliens. 1
b Three days later, there was a postcard ☐   **d** One alien said, 'We're lost!' ☐
for him.

11 Write the second part of Connor's story. Use the questions to help you.

1 What did Jake see? Where were they? How did Jake feel?
Jake saw _____
_____
_____

2 What did the aliens ask Jake? What did Jake say? Where did they want to go?
An alien asked, 'Where _____
_____
_____

3 Did Jake dream about the aliens? What happened three days later? Was it a dream?
Jake went to bed and _____
_____
_____

12 (3:10) Listen and circle the sounds you hear. Then complete the sentence.

1 sh   sw   **3** sh   sc
2 sc   sw   **4** sh   sw

Why are the ¹__arks ²__imming?
They're ³__ared of the small fi ⁴__ !

13 **Read and choose.**

1   Where does Serena go?
    a to the nature museum   **b** (to the underground river)   **c** home
2   What are the guards doing?
    a watching the show   **b** watching Serena   **c** sleeping
3   What does Serena find?
    a Champ   **b** a cage   **c** the time machine
4   Who is in a cage?
    a Zero Zendell   **b** Champ   **c** the guards

14 **Write the words. Then choose and label the pictures.**

1   txecide   _excited_   3   soiyn   _____   5   docl   _____
2   twe   _____   4   dscear   _____

They're ___excited___.

She's _____ and _____.

They're _____.

They're _____.

15 **Look at page 8. Find and write. Then answer.**

D E S N G R R H

W Z E Z E   Z O Z S   Z E Z E Z A   Z 0 ?

_____
_____
_____
_____

16 Read the clues. Complete the crossword.

Clues:

across

1 When you're in space your body is **?**

2 & 3 The names of the first two men on the Moon. **?** Armstrong and **?** Aldrin.

4 Jupiter is nearer the Sun than this planet.

down

1 Astronauts sleep in these.

2 The name of the first man in space.

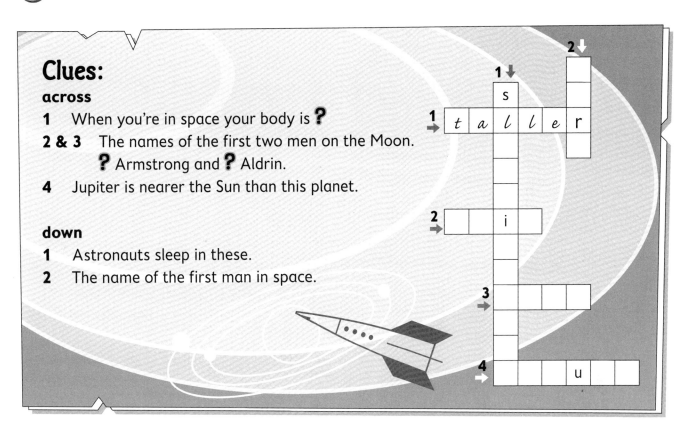

17 Can you remember the planets? Look at this sentence to help you. Say it with a friend.

Most Very Educated Monkeys Just Sleep Under Newspapers

18 Write another sentence to help you remember the planets.

_____

19 Look and write.

Wh- questions

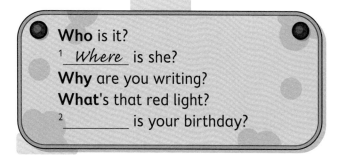

Who is it?
1 _Where_ is she?
Why are you writing?
What's that red light?
2 _____ is your birthday?

Comparing two things

One or two syllables	Three syllables or more
scary → 3 _____ than	frightening → more 7 _frightening_ than
easy → 4 _____ than	complicated → 8 _____ complicated **than**
small → 5 _____ than	exciting → more 9 _____ than
big → 6 _____ than	intelligent → more 10 _____ than

_My_ book is more interesting than _his_ book!

20 (3:13) **Complete the sentences. Use these words. Then listen and check.**

tall   complicated   scary   small   exciting   old

1 I'm _____taller_____ than my brother. He's very short.
2 Trampolining is _____ than doing homework. I love it!
3 My homework was _____ than your homework. Your homework was easy.
4 Thrillers are _____ than cartoons.
5 Those boys are _____ than us. They're fifteen!
6 Their bikes are _____ than our bikes. Our bikes are big.

21 Complete the Unit Quiz.

I CAN DO IT!

Unit Quiz ? ? ? ? ? ?

1 What can you use to look at the stars? _____

2 Name a job in space. _____

3 Name three long adjectives. **a** _____ **b** _____ **c** _____

4 Can you remember two facts about space?

_____

_____

22 Compare two of your friends.

My friend _____ is _____ than _____

_____

_____

_____

_____

_____

I CAN

☺ ☺ ☹

★ talk about space and aliens.

★ ask questions using *Who, Where, Why, What, When*.

★ use some long adjectives to compare things.

★ read, understand and listen to stories.

★ spell and say the /sm/, /st/, /sw/, /sk/, /sp/ and /ʃ/ sounds.

★ read and understand some facts about space.

8 Environment

1 Look and write.

> paper recycle switch off reuse rubbish

1 recycle the
_____ _paper_____

2 collect the
_____

3 _____
the bottles

4 _____
the bags

5 _____
the lights

2 Look at the chart and complete.

1 ___*Five*___ people always reuse bags.
2 _____ people usually reuse bags.
3 _____ people sometimes reuse bags.
4 _____ people never reuse bags.
5 The total number of people was _____.

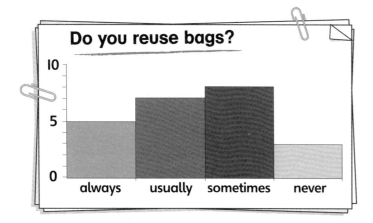

3 Ask and complete the chart for your class. Then write sentences.

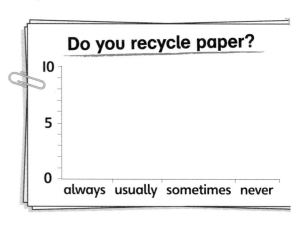

1 _____
2 _____
3 _____
4 _____

4 (3:19) **Look at Tom's plans for next week. Listen and complete.**

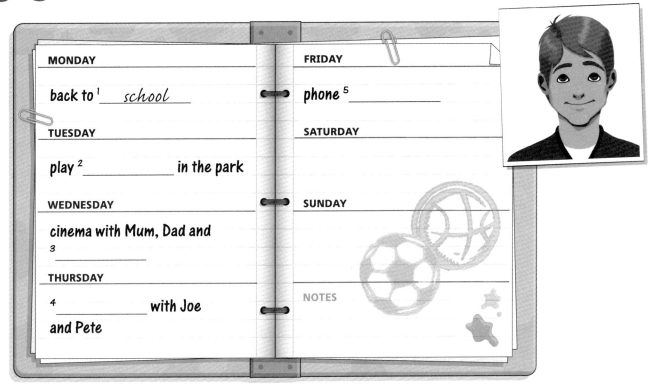

MONDAY

back to ¹ _school_

TUESDAY

play ² _____ in the park

WEDNESDAY

cinema with Mum, Dad and
³ _____

THURSDAY

⁴ _____ with Joe
and Pete

FRIDAY

phone ⁵ _____

SATURDAY

SUNDAY

NOTES

5 **Ask and answer. Then ask two more questions.**

1 park/Tuesday
2 phone/Joe/Friday

3 cinema/Thursday
4 pizza/Thursday

A: Is Tom going to play football in the park on Tuesday? **B:** Yes, he is.

6 **Write about your plans for next week. Make sentences, then tell a friend.**

On Monday, I'm going to _____
_____
_____
_____
_____
_____
_____
_____

7 Find six words. Then complete the sentences.

1 Monkeys ___chatter___ in the trees. They're very noisy!
2 The food in Argentina was _____. I loved it.
3 The Pacific is the largest _____ in the world.
4 What a big forest! There are trees _____!
5 Egypt is very dry but it's got _____ beaches.
6 New York is a big _____ in the USA.

8 3:22 Listen and write the names.

Mike   Monty   Max   Martin

9 There is one true sentence. Correct the false sentences.

1 Monty is the oldest.
2 Mike isn't the tallest.
3 Max is taller than Martin.
4 Max is the most intelligent.
5 Mike is the dirtiest.

10 (3:25) **Listen and answer.**

1 What's special about tomorrow? _____

2 What's Niki going to make? _____

3 What does Niki want from Molly? _____

11 (3:26) **Listen again and complete.**

Hi Molly,

It's Niki. Your plans for tomorrow sound fun! My class at school is going to have a Green Day. We're going to put all the ¹ _rubbish_ into different recycling bins and then we're going to make Green Day posters for school. I'm going to collect some ² _____ from home and other people are going to bring paper, ³ _____ and ⁴ _____. We're going to be the ⁵ _____ school in our town! Then, we're all going to walk or cycle home – no ⁶ _____ or ⁷ _____. I love cycling so I'm very happy. I'm going to like Green Day. Oh, and can I have your bike?

Thanks!

12 (3:27) **Look and complete. Then listen and check.**

1 I always have a ____shower____ at seven o'clock.

2 There were a lot of _____ in the sea.

3 The _____ is the fastest animal on the planet.

4 I love going to the _____ in the summer.

5 They usually have _____ at one o'clock.

6 She's very _____. She doesn't like talking to people.

13 🔊 3:29 **Listen and match. Who said it?**

1 Where were you?
2 We went to the year 2210!
3 There are no real pets in the future.
4 He was in a cage.
5 We need to look after our animals.

14 **Read and choose, or write your own answer.**

1 I think Marta is:
  a brave.
  b kind.
  c _____
2 I think Zero is:
  a mean.
  b scary.
  c _____
3 My favourite character is:
  a Champ.
  b Serena.
  c Marta.
  d _____
4 I think the story was:
  a exciting.
  b interesting.
  c _____

15 **Look at page 8. Find and write. Then find out.**

D D H A N D O H P T

WHAT HAPPENED TO THE DODO?

_____
_____
_____
_____
_____

16 (3:31) Read and choose. Then listen and check.

Our amazing world QUIZ

1 Mount Fuji is a famous **?**

| a forest. | c river. |
| b lake. | d volcano. |

2 The Nile passes through **?** countries.

| a twelve | c nineteen |
| b ten | d nine |

3 Australia is the **?** island in the world.

| a biggest | c fastest |
| b smallest | d highest |

4 Angel Falls is the **?** waterfall in the world.

| a slowest | c highest |
| b cleanest | d smallest |

17 Find out more facts. Write two quiz questions for a friend. Then ask and answer.

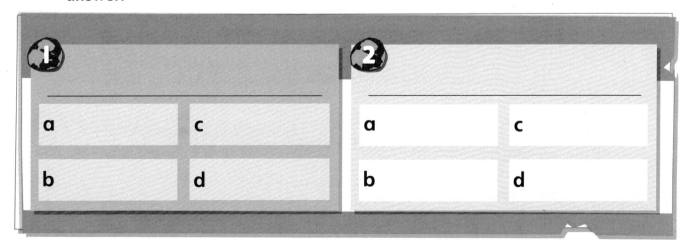

1 _____

| a | c |
| b | d |

2 _____

| a | c |
| b | d |

18 Read and write.

Talking about plans

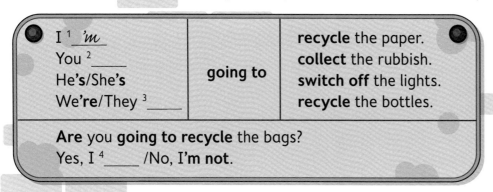

I ¹ _'m_ You ² ____ He**'s**/She**'s** We**'re**/They ³ ____	**going to**	**recycle** the paper. **collect** the rubbish. **switch off** the lights. **recycle** the bottles.
Are you **going to recycle** the bags? Yes, I ⁴ ____ /No, **I'm not**.		

Comparing three or more things

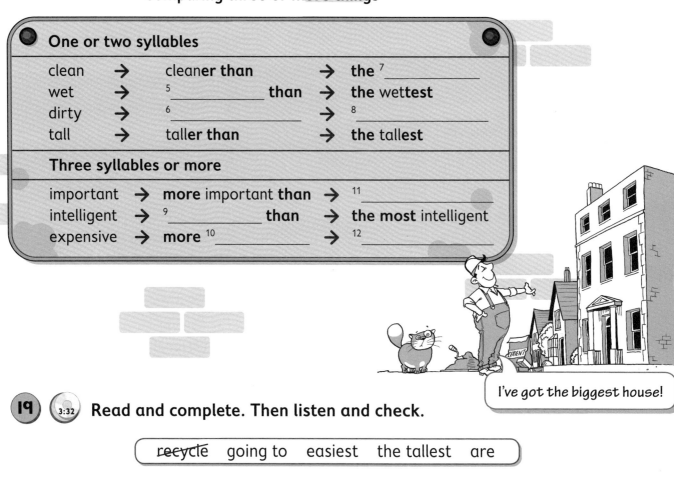

One or two syllables

clean	→	clea**n**er **than**	→	the ⁷ _____
wet	→	⁵ _____ **than**	→	the wet**test**
dirty	→	⁶ _____	→	⁸ _____
tall	→	tall**er than**	→	the tall**est**

Three syllables or more

important	→	**more** important **than**	→	¹¹_____
intelligent	→	⁹ _____ **than**	→	**the most** intelligent
expensive	→	**more** ¹⁰_____	→	¹²_____

I've got the biggest house!

19 🔊 3:32 Read and complete. Then listen and check.

recycle   going to   easiest   the tallest   are

1 Flo is going to __*recycle*__ the bottles.
2 Tom and Flo _____ going to visit their granny.
3 Tom is _____ phone Felipe next week.
4 I am _____ in my family.
5 English is the _____ subject in school!

I CAN DO IT!

20 **Complete the Unit Quiz.**

Unit Quiz

1 Complete the words.
a collect the _r_ _ _ _ _ _ _ _ _   c _r_ _ _ _ _ _ the bags
b switch off the _ _ _ _ _ _ _ _ _s   d _r_ _ _ _y_ _ _ _ the bottles

2 Order the question.

(you) (play) (are) (to) (on) (Saturday) (going) (football)

_____

3 Write your answer. _____

4 Look at the two sentences. Write *funnier than* or *the funniest*.
a My sister is _____ my brother. She makes me laugh.
b My grandad is _____. Nobody is funnier!

21 **Write about your plans.**

At the weekend, I'm going to _____

Next week, I'm going _____

Next year, I'm _____

22 **Describe your family. Who is the tallest/shortest/funniest/fastest?**

_____

_____

_____

I CAN

☺ ☺ ☹

★ talk about saving the environment.
★ talk about plans.
★ compare three or more things.
★ do a quiz about the environment.
★ spell and say the /tʃ/ and /ʃ/ sounds.
★ read and understand some facts about our world.

Christmas

1 Order the letters. Then find the mystery word.

1 cbaebrue

2 piatañ

3 tnpeerss

4 aotg

5 twsese

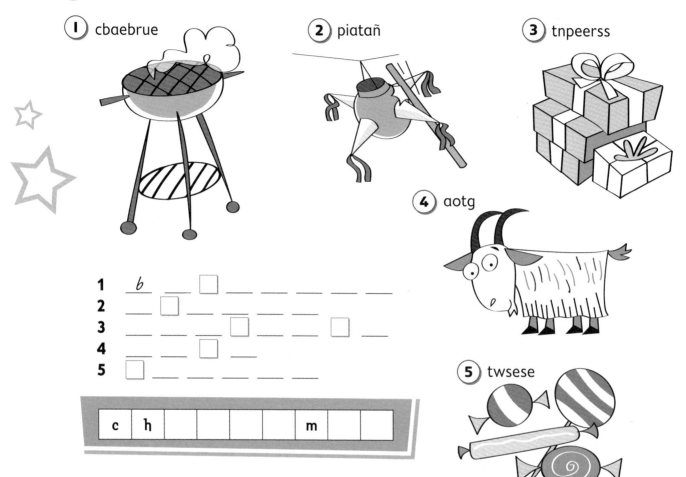

1 _b_ __ ☐ __ __ __ __ __ __
2 __ ☐ __ __ __ __ __
3 __ __ __ ☐ __ __ ☐ __
4 __ __ ☐ __ __
5 ☐ __ __ __ __ __ __ __

c	h					m		

2 Match.

1 This means 'Happy Christmas' in Swedish.
2 I like going here for a barbecue.
3 This animal gives presents in Sweden.
4 Children in Mexico hit this to get sweets.
5 This means 'Happy Christmas' in Spanish.

a The beach.
b *Feliz Navidad.*
c A *piñata.*
d *God Jul!*
e A goat.

3 Write about Christmas or another festival in your country.

_____

_____

_____

_____

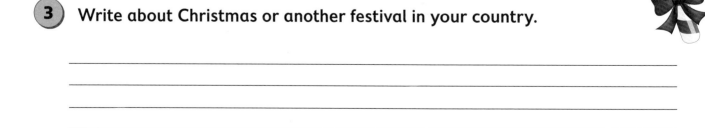

New Year

1 Find the words. Which four things can you see? Write.

| fireworks | dragon | lamp | parade | midnight | ~~New Year~~ | party | Diwali |

w	f	y	j	d	b	d	o	t
m	i	d	n	i	g	h	t	l
s	r	q	m	w	n	i	w	p
d	e	r	l	a	o	n	y	a
r	w	r	a	l	p	e	u	r
a	o	a	m	i	a	j	b	a
g	r	t	p	e	r	f	c	d
o	k	l	s	m	t	r	w	e
n	s	n	e	w	y	e	a	r

a

b

_____

c

_____

d

_____

2 Complete with words from Activity 1.

1 ___New Year___ is on 1st January every year.
2 I like watching _____ at the town square on 31st December.
3 New Year in India is called _____.
4 People in Spain eat grapes at _____ to celebrate New Year.
5 In China, dancers wear _____ costumes at New Year.

3 Find and write questions. Then write the answers.

1 (in) (New) (when) (Year) (is) (Britain)
_____*When is New Year in Britain?*_____   _____*1st January*_____

2 (costumes) (where) (people) (do) (dragon) (wear)
_____   _____

3 (days) (Diwali) (many) (how) (is)
_____   _____

4 (people) (do) (where) (in) (New Year) (October) (celebrate)
_____   _____

Word list

1
Adventure camp

adventurer
bring
buildings
calm
chief
compass
cover our heads
dollar
funfair
keep out the rain
lay out the bed
mountaineer
pitch a tent
put in the pegs
rucksack
sleeping bag
time machine
torch
yoga

I **love** play**ing** (basketball).
I'm good at (swim**ming**).
We**'re reading** (a compass).

2
Wild animals

cage
camouflage
centimetres
chameleon
cheetah
females
flies
heavy
joey
kilograms
koala
lemur
males
metres
museum
otter
panther
point (1.8)
reserve
rhino
seal
slow
snake
sponsor
tiger
tortoise
turns (red)
turtle
valuable
whale

How (**heavy**) is it?
They're **bigger than** (my pet fish).

3
Where I live

airport
architect
behind
bench
between
castle
chimneys
cinema
city
clouds
ice cream van
in front of
library
near
next to
opposite
park
rain
rescue
robot
roof
shopping centre
sky
sunset
supermarket
swimming pool
town
village

Do you **want to** (**watch** it with me)?
I **don't want to** (**waste** my time).
I **want to** (**watch** the sun).

4
Good days

climbed
competition
cooked
curry
drop (the ball)
dropped
filmed
fish and chips
joined
journey
lock
loved
miss (the bus)
omelette
onstage
open (a lunchbox)
pack (my bag)
paddled
paella
pass (a test)
played
remember (my juice)
roof
sailed
sailor
solo
spaghetti
storm
tasty
wanted
wedding

I/He **didn't** (**ask** why).

5
Trips

aquarium
big wheel
boating lake
carousel
dodgems
flag
harbour
mini-golf
museum
palace
rollercoaster
sandy
slap (on a hat)
slip (on some
 clothes)
slop (on the sun
 cream)
surfboard
theatre
theme park
underground
water park

Did you **go** to
 (the museum)?
Did you **like**
 (the big wheel)?
Yes, I **did**./
 No, I **didn't**.

6
Arts

blues
brought
cartoon
comedy
concert
crossed
drum
flashing
guitar
habits
had
harmonica
heard
jazz
made
musical
neat
piano
pop
read
rock
romance
saved
saw
saxophone
sci-fi
sloppy
stole
stripes
thriller
violin
wrote
zebra

Did you **hear**
 (the piano)?

7
Space

alien
amazing
astronaut
complicated
disgusting
field
frightening
intelligent
land
Moon
planet
solar system
spaceship
star
telescope
woke up

Travel in space is
 more (**exciting**)
 than travel on
 Earth.
What ...?
When ...?
Where ...?
Who ...?
Why ...?

8
Environment

better
chatter
cleaner
collect (the
 rubbish)
continent
everywhere
kinder
more important
north
ocean
on foot
recycle (the
 paper/bottles)
reuse (the bags)
south
switch off (the
 lights)
take
taller
the cleanest
the kindest
the most
 important
the tallest
throw
wonderful

Are you **going
 to help**?
Yes, I **am**./No,
 I'**m not**.
I'**m going to**
 (**recycle** the
 bottles).

Wider World

Camping around the world

cabin
deer
lizards
motorbike
peaks
sandy
squirrels
volcanic

Our homes

fishing
flat
harbour
million
restaurants
sailing
sports centre
taekwondo
volleyball

Our holidays

ancient
built
emperor
hot-air balloon
lost
married
ruins
sundial
tombs
wife

World instruments

bandoneón
buttons
djembe drums
notes
pulls
pushes
shamisen
skin
strings
tango
wood

Festival

Christmas

barbecue
decorate
fall
pick up
stick

New Year

dragon costume
grapes
midnight
oil lamps
parades